PREPARATION OF THE COMING KING

PASTOR REGINA C. BRENT

CLAY BRIDGES
PRESS

Preparation of the Coming King

Copyright © 2018 by Pastor Regina C. Brent

Published by Clay Bridges Press in Houston, TX.

Scripture quotations marked (KJV) are taken from the King James Version (KJV): King James Version, public domain.

Scripture quotations marked (GNB) are taken from the Good News Bible © 1994 published by the Bible Societies/HarperCollins Publishers Ltd UK, Good News Bible © American Bible Society 1966, 1971, 1976, 1992. Used with permission.

The Holy Bible New International Version (NIV) Copyright © 1973, 1978, 1984, 2011 by Biblica, Inc. TM used by permission. All rights reserved worldwide.

Publication made possible through
Extended Hands of Jesus Ministry
COPYRIGHT #Txu 617-690 DATED September 18, 1996

First Revision September 10, 1996
Second Revision February 27, 2007
Third Revision February 27, 2017
Fourth Revision March 20, 2018
Fifth Revision, May 21, 2018

eISBN-10: 1-939815-44-4 | eISBN-13: 978-1-939815-44-6
ISBN-10: 1-939815-43-6 | ISBN-13: 978-1-939815-43-9

Special Sales: Most Clay Bridges Press titles are available in special quantity discounts. Custom imprinting or excerpting can also be done to fit special needs. Contact Clay Bridges Press at info@claybridgespress.com.

Joel 2:15-16 (NIV)

"Blow the trumpet in Zion, declare a holy fast, call a sacred assembly. Gather the people, consecrate the assembly; bring together the elders, gather the children, those nursing at the breast. Let the Bridegroom leave His room and the bride her chamber."

To the Body of Christ—a bride who looks forward to her wedding day. In preparing for His coming, may she be found without blemish, waiting in earnest expectation for a groom who is worthy of her eternal love, praise, and honor. This book is dedicated to you.

TABLE OF CONTENTS

PREFACE

T he Lord placed within my spirit years ago that there is
much work to be done in the kingdom. Presently, He is
sanctifying His church. It is all a part of the preparation for
the coming of our Lord and Savior Jesus Christ. The church does
not have time to idly sit by and wait it out. He also showed me that
He is doing heart surgery in the Spirit on His body. He said to me,
"My heart, My heart!" God's heart is for lost souls.

In Matthew 5:7 Jesus said, *"Blessed are the merciful for they will
be shown mercy."* (NIV) God's mercies are new every morning; so
should it be with His people. We are Christ's representatives here
on earth. Evangelization is needed in so many areas, corporations,
prison ministries, the sick, the backslider, the homeless, and yes,
even our own families. While God is purifying His church and
cleansing us from our sins, so we must in turn speak this same
salvation message to those bound by the evil one. Salvation is
calling out and the heavens are waiting for us to move. There are
no exceptions. We need to make disciples of new converts. We
no longer have the option of pointing fingers and arguing over
doctrine.

We must act now!

The Son of Man will come in glory sitting on His glorious

throne. All nations will assemble before Him. He will separate them one from the other as the shepherd separates the sheep from the goats. The sheep are on His right, the goats on His left. It is time to feed the hungry, to give drink to those who are thirsty, it is time to put on robes of righteousness, it is time to visit people who are sick and in prison.

When the Lord returns, He will separate the sheep from the goats. He will gather His sheep for He knows them by name and counts them as His own. Goats tend to be contentious and warlike toward sheep. God will dismiss them into the hands of the devil and his angels. (Matthew 25:31-46 NIV).

Jesus' promises kingdom inheritance to those who are:

1. Hospitable: Those whose hearts are open to everyone and those who are willing to love and welcome them; not just in a home, but in God's kingdom. They are sheep who are moved with compassion to serve God and their fellow man and has a desire to follow God's will and commands.

2. Those who are hungry; not only for food but for His righteousness.

3. Those who are thirsty; not just for drink but for His living waters.

4. Those who are in need of clothes: Garments to cover their nakedness and heavenly garments supplied by God.

5. In sickness: Those who would comfort and encourage others in love and prayers.

6. In prison: Those who are incarcerated and in spiritual bondage.

We have seen evidence in these end times of atheists and others who are pushing their antichrist agenda of removing bibles and the Ten Commandments from state buildings; who are passing human laws by taking prayers out of our schools. God cannot be removed and He will not be silent. He has ears to hear and they are open to every prayer spoken by His people. Stand, therefore, firm in your faith and remain steadfast and immovable.

Rise up! The lost are awaiting God's plan and purpose.

Rise up as we see the day approaching . . .

Time waits for no one and the clock is ticking. Preparation is a process and the Lord says no one knows the day or the hour of His coming. This book compares God's plan for man and lays out His final plan to gather His people together for that great day. God's word and prayer sustains us throughout our lives, guides us in the right direction, and helps us to remain steadfast until God's people receive their rightful inheritance.

We were born to fly; to reach for the sky; not stumble in the dark and miss the mark. Earthbound citizens weary in labor; experience pain and suffering, war and famine; and at the end of it all, we are gone like the wind of breath that once gave us life.

We were born to be lights in the sky with a twinkle in our eye; walking with God Who is ever nigh. I want no sad bad ending in my life story; only God and His hope of glory.

Word from the Lord – May 21, 2018 –

"Surely I am the Waymaker. I will clear a path for My people to succeed and render thanksgiving unto their God. The path of righteousness was given sacrificially from My Son; now I am clearing a new path void of hindrances and encumbrances. The enemy will not be able to penetrate or infiltrate it. Rejoice O people of Zion! Let joy spring forth like a fountain from your heart. I am paving new highways that will stand up to the pressure and smooth the way for My coming."

God has been opening up a way for His children since the time of Creation and the journey through the Red Sea and the wilderness. He has revealed Himself as a God of miracles, signs, and wonders; as a Healer and Way Maker; as love, peace, and joy; as Provider and Protector; as Shepherd and Teacher; Defender and Friend. He is our only salvation and He is coming soon.

- The alarm is sounding!
- Signs and wonders fill the skies.
- Time is calling us to a sacred assembly.
- The sound of His coming is in the wind.
- Truth in prophecy is being revealed.

Are you prepared?

INTRODUCTION

Prophecy is unfolding as we move forward to a great expectation; the arrival of our soon coming King, the Lord Jesus Christ.

From the time of the chosen people of God in the Old Testament and in the books of Daniel and Isaiah to the minor prophets moving prophecy forward in time to the birth and resurrection of our Lord Jesus Christ, God has been preparing the world for His second coming. Are we prepared? Do we know what to expect or what God expects of us? I pray that this book will give you some insight into these answers.

Life is all about preparation –

- When we have an appointment, we decide upon a time and set the alarm clock. We then get up early enough to take a shower and get dressed and hope we make it there on time.

- When we are seriously ill, we prepare ourselves to go the hospital and bring our insurance card ready to fill out paperwork. Before the doctors perform the surgery, they must consult with their patients, check x-rays and make a diagnosis.

- When we plan a vacation, we prepare by contacting travel agencies or airlines with a full itinerary. We then make the reservations for travel and hotel.

- When we graduate from High School, we have to prepare by first writing letters to several universities to see which college will accept our application.

- When we want to apply for a job, we must prepare by writing a resume with our personal information, educational status and any prior experience we may have qualifying us for that particular position.

Preparation means positioning ourselves to move ahead. The signs Jesus spoke about in the gospel are very apparent in this age. At this point in time, God is more interested in how we are to prepare ourselves for His second coming. God is sounding an alarm and He wants us to get dressed and ready to live with Him throughout eternity.

1

NEW BIRTH

We are destined to be born twice in this life: a physical birth and spiritual birth with the newness of life by our faith, confession, repentance, and acceptance through our Lord and Savior Jesus Christ.

A husband and wife must make a mutual decision to have children and then prepare a time and season beforehand. Sometimes it just happens and surprises both the mother and the father. The next step is to look at their budget to see if they are financially able to support the child and will they be able to sacrifice time, money, school, provide clothes and food, and prepare to always be in a position to watch out for their safety and protection. *Physical*: A woman knows her own body the way God knows His Bride (the Body of Christ). When a woman's water breaks, she must prepare herself for delivery of her new born.

God wants us to make a decision; the most important decision of our lives. He wants us to be born again into a covenant relationship of marriage. When God makes a covenant, it is sealed and kept throughout eternity. He sacrificed His Son on the cross as atonement for our sins and we are redeemed by the cross of

Jesus Christ. He provides for us, protects us, love and instructs us; but most of all, He wants to prepare us for His arrival.

In preparation for the coming of the Lord, there must not only be a 'new birth' but we must be set free from the captivity of this world system including all rebellion against God's authority and man's and we must rid ourselves of sin and lawlessness.

Is the Body of Christ prepared to work with God; to build up people and step out in faith to save a lost world?

The word of the Lord on Tuesday, March 27, 2018 –

"The weak have need of a Savior. Be on hand to help. Give what I have given to you 'mercy'. Break free from all stumbling blocks that will keep you away from your work in My kingdom. When I call for you, be ready to obey My will and purpose for you. For God is able to silence the threat of war and cause lions to be docile. This unruly generation shall be tamed and I shall accomplish this in the time of My glory."

2
SETTING THE
CAPTIVES FREE

Isaiah 61:1-3 (KJV)

God is all about setting people free; that is why He chose Moses to deliver His people out of the bondage of Egypt to worship Him on His holy mountain where He gave them His laws and commands and advanced them forward towards the promised land of milk and honey.

He released Abraham from his family for the future covenant and promise of blessing upon his seed to make him the father of all nations. (Gen. 17:4 NIV).

He chose Esther to fast and pray so that the Jews would not perish. As a result, the Jewish nation was set free from death and the grave. (Esther chapter's 3-7 NIV).

Daniel, when he was held captive by the Babylonians, was required to abide by the King's law and commands but God granted him favor with the Commander of the Officials. (Daniel chapter 1 NIV).

He chose Jonah to go to Nineveh with His message to set the people free from sin and corruption. (Jonah chapter 1 NIV).

Jesus came to set men free by teaching and preaching His gospel. He freed people from sickness, sin, and disease and sacrificed Himself on the cross for our salvation. Redemption is ours today and our sins are washed away. All curses have been removed.

When we commit a crime, we must prepare to pay the penalty by going to jail and appearing before a judge. The penalty of sin is death but Jesus Christ stood in our place and we are redeemed because of His perfect work on the cross.

Prison is a place of confinement where you reap what you have sown in this life. It has limited space and you may have to share that space with someone else who has committed a crime of his own making. You are isolated from the rest of the world, including your family. Being held captive restricts your movements and you have to come under the authority of others who make sure you do not step out of line. You left one form of bondage to get into an even stricter form of bondage. Sin does that to an individual. It separates us from God and His family. But give praise to God; for He is a God of second chances and He is able to set us free from all captivity.

There are many of God's people today that are setting captives free through the Spirit of God by the cleansing of the word; people who are making a difference. I have a sister in Christ who, years ago, was called to third ward in Houston, Texas to bring prostitutes and drug addicts to the Lord. She has a call to deliver and set free those bound by the devil. She went into crack houses not fearing for her life bringing the word of God to lost souls. She cooked meals on Sundays for the poor. She always says, "God's heart is for lost souls."

Every year as America celebrates the Fourth of July as their day of Independence, God and all the hosts of heaven celebrate our freedom when we repent of our sins and choose life by accepting the Lord Jesus Christ as our Lord and Savior. This is the most important first step in preparing to meet the King.

3

MY FIRST MINISTRY

1987

We build prisons of our own when we set up bars between our heart and God's.

My first ministry came out of the Lord's word in Isaiah 61:1 KJV and that is to 'Set the Captives Free'. Jesus recited this same scripture of Isaiah in Luke 4:18-19 (KJV) at a synagogue in Nazareth; and said on the same day the scripture would be fulfilled in their hearing. It is still being fulfilled today by missionaries, Christian churches, and ministries all over the world. They will continue to fulfill this commission set forth by Jesus Christ until the Lord returns.

On January 27, 1988, I had written a paper entitled, "Is the Prison Ministry for You?" It was a recruiting tool when I was Prison Ministry Leader for the Church of Christ in the Houston area. The organization was called *Christ Prison Fellowship*. They gathered a few people from several Churches of Christ in the

Houston area and met in one location. The organization itself was based in the Dallas area. My past experience has helped me to develop an agape love, not only for the lost, but also for God's people. My first ministry was quite a challenge and very unpopular at the time. A small portion of what I mentioned in my paper is given below (the last names of these inmates are not given for purposes of anonymity to those who were incarcerated at the time of this writing):

"Is the Prison Ministry for You?"

It is no secret to anyone that Texas prisons are overcrowded and new facilities are being built to compensate for this problem by the state. In today's world, people are more concerned with the economy, job security, and so on to really get involved in any ministry that is spiritually worth while. God really has to equip you for this particular kind of ministry. I was not prepared for what I had to take on. A couple at my church recommended me for this ministry at a time when Watergate was fresh in the minds of the American people. This was a new ministry in the Body of Christ and a not so popular one.

On our first trip of the New Year to Huntsville, a member of our group expressed his view about the ministry. He said a member of his congregation approached him with a statement. "The Prison Ministry is not one of the church's priorities." He replied, "Is God's will a priority?" The Prison Ministry may not be for everyone, but scripture tells us that it should not be overlooked:

All of the earth's people will be gathered before God and His angels when He comes again as Lord and King. He will then divide them into 2 groups: The sheep on the right and the goats on the left. In verse 36, God positions Himself in the place of the needy here on earth as He speaks to the righteous. He said

8

He was naked and was clothed; sick and was cared for; and was visited in prison. In verse 45 He makes a final statement by saying that if we refuse to help the least of these, it is the same as refusing Him. (Matthew 25:31-36 GNB).

On this same note, a member of my congregation spoke with me about the Prison Ministry. She said, "How can you forgive those people for what they did?" I replied, "The same way Jesus forgave me when I was lost in sin."

As humans, our ways are not always humane so Romans 3:23 reminds us that we all fall short because of our sinful nature. Are we vicarious in the sense that we are pointing the finger at our brothers and sisters who do fall short? Christ Prison Fellowship has been instrumental in accomplishing this worthy task by introducing Christ into the lives of those who have never had the opportunity to study the word of God or those who knew the word of God but have gone astray. Jeremiah 18:6 speaks of a Potter (the Lord) who molds clay that is imperfect and reshapes it until it becomes a thing of beauty.

Institutional rehabilitation is beneficial in teaching occupational and educational skills that will be helpful to inmates who want to find proper employment once they are released from the prison system. Although these achievements are a basic necessity, they are physical and external in scope only. It is a fact that once the inmate is released into his or her same environment, they return back into the prison system like a vicious cycle. Jesus wants us to clean the inside of the cup. This ministry works on changing the whole person spiritually. First, from within so that when the inmate is free to enter the world outside, he may be a living example and testimony of the power of God and how He is able to change our lives. Second, he can become a witness to others about the life changing word of God and an acceptable contributing member of society. Third, he is able to seek a church suitable for his study so that he will continue to be discipled in God's word (accountability). (2 Corin. 5:17-21 KJV). Through such a ministry, they have become new men and women in Christ through the transforming power of the word of God.

What does one get out of prison visitation? This question can be answered by a series of four (4) memorable visits to the prison:

1. When I visited an inmate (we shall call him "V") at the Eastham Unit (a maximum-security prison), he informed me (just as all the previous inmates I had visited) that his family had completely cut him off. He does not receive any letters or visits from family members. His father committed suicide and no one ever bothered to tell him until his cousin sent a newspaper clipping but yet..."V" remained a soldier for Christ. He never gave up his faith. On one particular visit, I told him about the problems I was experiencing with an accounting course and he immediately prayed for me that God would help me in my studies. I can testify today that God truly answered that prayer.

2. Another inmate named John at the Goree Unit said, "I am glad God sent me here because if I hadn't come, I would have never found Christ." This same inmate had me call his mother when I returned home. She told me that she prayed for God to send someone to speak to her son and thanked me for my visit. She also offered up prayers for my concern.

3. A former inmate who accompanied us on our last trip made a comment to everyone visiting. He conveyed his feelings about how the ministry helped him during his term in prison. He said, "You were kind enough to take the time to visit someone who was an outcast to society,

and it changed my life." He continued to say that he saw Christ through us during our visits.

4. In November of 1987, four inmates testified about their love for the Lord and cited scriptures in the prison chapel. One of the inmates commented that we shouldn't be selfish with our gifts or with what we have learned about the word of God and that Jesus wanted us to share his word in fellowship with other Christians. Just as God sent him there for a reason, He also sent us for the same reason.

The inmates loved to sing Amazing Grace.

Many of these prisoners are wealthy individuals, elected officials, preachers, and in some cases, police officers. So as you can see, they are not just people from poverty-stricken areas of the city, not all alcoholics, and not all drug addicts although, they do make up a large majority of people being incarcerated. Christians inside continue to be scrutinized and persecuted by other inmates because of their faith. The importance of these visits is to reinforce that faith by fellowshipping with them and letting them know that they are not alone in their struggle, in their prayers, or in their influence on others within the prison to be living examples of the power of God. Is this ministry for you?

I prayed this paper would touch the hearts of the people in my church assembly.

We are never to fear what we must suffer as servants of God. If we just remain faithful until death, we will receive the crown of life. (Rev. 2:10 NIV).

Why did the word of God place so much emphasis on setting captives and prisoners free? Liberty and freedom to serve God is as important and vital today as it was during the time of Moses and the exodus of the people of Israel. Freedom rests in the Spirit of the Lord. (2 Corin. 3:17 GNB).

For the sake of the gospel was another reason why there is so much emphasis on setting the captives free. Let's recall the lives of the Apostle Paul and Peter. Paul called himself '*a prisoner of Jesus Christ*'. He was placed in prison for preaching the gospel and although confined, he was committed to doing the will of God no matter what the cost. Paul and Silas were placed in prison and at midnight, worship and prayer went up to God. God then caused an earthquake which shook the foundations of that prison; the doors opened and chains fell off all of the prisoners. (Acts 16:25-26 GNB). An Angel of the Lord appeared to Peter while he was in prison and he was released prompted by the fervent prayers of Believers in Acts 12:5-14 (KJV).

There were a few prisons that would not allow us to take our bibles inside. Now we know why we must study the word of God and hold it in our hearts and practice memory verses. For the last few years certain groups have been working against God by not allowing people in our military and certain buildings within the city to keep bibles. The remedy for that is to buy a bible and study it on your own or join a bible based church for a more extensive study.

Many of God's people are saved but not delivered. Discipleship after conversion is so crucial in the Body of Christ. Sometimes the old man appears with the same old habits. Jesus said, *"No one sews a patch of unshrunk cloth on an old garment, for the patch will pull away from the garment, making the tear worse. Neither do men pour new wine into old wineskins."* (Matt 9:16-17 NIV).

The riches of the kingdom given by God is to not only to be accepted and desired which would ultimately transform us from our former rebellious and sinful ways but it is also to be treasured in our open hearts of adoration and commitment to our King. It is then that we are truly delivered.

Eventually, the Lord moved me out of the Prison Ministry after about nine (9) years into another church. I became an intercessor and was asked to join the Altar Ministry. One Sunday, during praise and worship, God told me that He was giving me a Deliverance Ministry and subsequently gave me my own prayer group.

This same prayer group, over the years, has developed into a ministry called, 'Extended Hands of Jesus' of which I am founder and pastor. Our first order of business is prayer. We are intercessors standing in the gap for ministers of the gospel and the body of Christ of all denominations and all nations. My prayer group has developed into a resource center for various biblical studies and research materials for the Body of Christ. We have on-line weekly newsletters and *In This Prophetic Age* write-ups on current events. We communicate with kingdom connections in various parts of the United States. We were faithful in little and God made the increase.

1

A PERSONAL VIEW

My personal goal in life has always been related to the last paragraph that is cited in the book of James Chapter 5:19-20 (GNB) which is to bring back truth to those who wander from it.

In 1992, God gave me a vision of baby carriages lined up in a row along a narrow dirt road. They were of all shapes and sizes. When I looked inside there was one large piece of steak. I asked the question, "What is the food for"? A voice said to me, "For the wedding." The next morning these two scriptures were given to me: I Corin 2:10-11 (KJV) – The Spirit searches and reveals the deep things of God; and I Corin. 3:12-13 (KJV) – we have not received the spirit of the world but of God. As a result, we do not speak with man's wisdom but by the Spirit of God. We must move from beyond milk and get into the meat of God's word. The Body of Christ must mature so we can become equipped for the building up of God's kingdom. (Ephes. 4:10-12 NIV).

Preparation cannot be made complete without the meat of the word.

The Lord made sure I had a good foundation in His word and I received that from the Church of Christ. Ultimately, I started studying on my own and, as the Spirit led and gave revelation, I began writing. He spoke to me out of Isa. 42:9 KJV. I was to forget the past and move into what His plans were for me now and in the future. The Body of Christ cannot stay on milk forever; we must grow and move forward into maturity growing in wisdom. We all must be held accountable. We all must know God, His character, His will, and purpose. The Body of Christ must have vision of where God is taking them.

One way God speaks to us, besides through the guidance of His Holy Spirit, is through His word. Jesus said that this world will pass away but the word of God shall never pass away. (Matthew 24:35 KJV). If the Word of God is written on your heart and you are truly rooted and grounded in His word; you will receive God's purpose and vision for your own life.

We must always be prepared for a word in due season (I believe whether it is giving a word or receiving one). Preach the word! *Be ready with the word as opportunity opens up whether it is convenient or inconvenient. (2 Tim. 4:2 GNB). In my life, there were times when the Lord brought people my way or vice versa. God always finds a way. He is the Way Maker. The word will find you right where you are. Romans 13:11 NIV says, ". . . wake up from your slumber, because our salvation is nearer now than when we first believed."*

5

COMPARISON. MAN'S QUEST AND GOD'S CHOICE

Humans teach, study, and search for other galaxies, stars and planets. Why can't we pursue and make an effort in our search for God and His righteousness? For the first time, tourists will pay to fly to outer space in 2018. Some would pay millions of dollars to travel into outer space. It is alright to study the stars; even Kings followed the star of Bethlehem which led them to Jesus Christ. It is another thing when we start worshipping the stars; then it becomes idolatry. (Deut. 4:19). I don't know about you, but I would rather be traveling into the heavens when the Lord decides to take me home and the passage is free of charge.

God is still calling Kings and nations to Jesus Christ to prepare for His coming. Man has always searched for new lands and new territories. God gave the people of Israel new lands and new territories as an inheritance. Even now Russia's invasion of eastern Ukraine, China building islands in the South Sea, and ISIS has a hunger for invading and conquering new territory. Yet, the word of God tells us that everything in the earth and all its fullness belongs to the Lord.

America searches for fantasy lands through videos, movies, and new technology. God searches for that one man of faith that will stand in the gap for others; that one man or woman who would say yes to His will and purpose.

We expect financial increase and returns on our investments and God wants a return on His Son's sacrifice and investment in our salvation. He atoned for our sins and has given us His Spirit. The word of God tells us to make ourselves a living sacrifice, holy and acceptable to Him.

Man searches for love in all the wrong places, they believe and listen to all the wrong voices. God is love and no love is greater than His. No other investment gives you so great a return as eternal life with God.

6

THE WORLD TODAY

Sometimes I feel as though the world is placed on a big warship and we are all passengers looking to the skies for the enemy, listening for gun fire, and waiting for a war to break out. Jesus said in the last days *"You will hear of wars and rumors of wars, but see to it that you are not alarmed."* (Matthew 24:6 NIV). The United States of America and North Korea is just one example.

Satan is the enemy of our soul and of this world. His heaviest infiltrations and attacks in this world are taking place in these world systems and institutions:

- Our Schools: Satan wants to steal the future of our children and cut off our generations by sowing death and violence. He is a destroyer of life, godly training and wisdom.

   In the late 1990's, my friend Toni (she has now gone on to be with the Lord) and I were on our way to Abundant Life Christian Center in LaMarque, Texas. We were passing through Santa Fe, Texas (where the recent shooting at a school occurred in May of 2018). She decided to stop and go into a store. As I waited in her pickup truck, I saw an open vision of someone shooting people (including my friend Toni) coming in and out of the store and there was blood everywhere. I was wide awake and could not believe what I saw. When Toni returned to the truck, I told her about my vision and that she is never to stop in Santa Fe, Texas or visit that store again. I believe the vision was prophetic of things to come. Please remember this city in your prayers. On June 19, 2000, the Supreme Court voted against students praying at the schools (football and other events) in the Santa Fe Independent School District. (See the history of Santa Fe, Texas on-line).

- Our Justice Systems: Through illegal entry, Satan wants to change God's laws of righteousness and transform them into an immoral and sinful, lawless society.

- Politics and Government: Abusive power of pride and greed are Satan's weapons. He wants to use certain people to sow lies, discord, bias, distractions and dissatisfaction within government authorities seated over nations and civil government.

- The Middle East: He wants to stir up violence by having people focus on their own selfish needs and beliefs rather than God's love and provision as given in His promises. Satan wants to replace love with hate. Decades of religious and territorial conflict; continuous war and death on all sides have fueled wars in the Middle East. Even as a teenager, I have seen former U.S. Presidents try to intervene in Middle Eastern affairs and peace agreements but have failed. It will take the God of Israel's hand to intervene on man's behalf to bring lasting peace to all nations. (Declare Psalm 96:1-10 KJV).

- Minds: Why would anyone want to turn over their mind to a thief and a lair? When we follow the devil's path instead of the Lord's, that is exactly what we are doing. When the word of God, pure love and truth, is absent from our minds and hearts, Satan fills it with deception. This is where Satan finds a position of power. If we are not careful, he will gain a foothold.

When the lives of man operates against the will and word of God and His divine nature, the world opens the door to Satan and his evil demons with evidence of rebellion and lawlessness. Creation must align itself with God's word as spoken forth by God at the beginning of creation.

Man tends to wait until tragedy hits and beg to ask the question, "Why?" They say, "Someone has to do something." They then grab hold of their picket signs marching through the streets of our cities relying on human will hoping for the best. God has already done something. The gospel must be poured into this generation and the generations to come opening up a way for man to come to the saving grace of our Lord and Savior Jesus Christ.

All we have to do is observe the evil condition in which this world is headed and remember the words of Jesus in Matt. 24:1-31 and the words written by the apostle Paul in 2 Tim. 3:1-5.

There are pleasant and peaceful times when I feel like I am in the clouds humbled before King Jesus waiting to hear what He will say. I talk to my sisters in Christ about how I get excited every time I think about His second return and all of the problems of the world just fade away.

Over the centuries, men wanted to settle their differences in several ways –

- When angered, they let their fists do the talking.
- Cowboys would rather wear an iron on their hip.
- Nations threaten nuclear war.
- Murder and mayhem.
- They curse and yell.
- Divided loyalties like political parties through elections.
- Compromise.
- Peace negotiations.
- Genuine love and forgiveness.

The political systems of this world have become so corrupt over the decades that people of the nations are no longer tolerable of its damaging effects in government. But we do have good news; the word of God says the government is upon His shoulders for He is the only wise God.

Everyone in this age from world leaders, religious leaders, and people of all nations are trying to find the worst in people. Sin has its name on everyone. We were all guilty before Jesus died on the cross. Unlike man, Jesus sees the best in us and wants to bless us with His salvation here and now by showing us the path to righteousness before the Lord comes again.

Differences are a challenge to resolve but not with God. Nothing is impossible for Him. He is a God of order. God is not a God who discriminates but communicates. His heart and love extends to the hated and wounded as well as the loving and caring.

Most men and women gamble their lives and livelihood away on sin and lawlessness, chips, cards, horses, and one-armed bandits. I'll take my chances on Jesus Christ, He is a sure bet.

Privacy has lost its way and theft has found its way into our identities and bank accounts through technology. Man invented computers and laptops for a more efficient way of keeping records and communicating but it has been used for both good and evil. I would rather communicate with God through His word and find increased treasure and a wealth of wisdom for my life. No one can steal that.

As long as we keep looking and relating to the world today, we will cease to have hope or peace. We are born to serve a Savior whose name is Jesus Christ. Prepare yourself to be introduced. We must keep in pace with God and move with His Spirit if we are ever going to survive in this world today with all the threats, racial hatred, religious hatred, wars, violence, drug use, human trafficking, etc.

Let's move forward into His divine plan for us in prophecy.

God is Ruler over Kings and nations and He has a plan of salvation that will prepare you for His glorious return. Why be concerned about the world and all of its turmoil when you are destined to follow the king whose kingdom is forever.

I have been talking to the Lord over the years telling Him that I want him and me to go for a ride together on horses when I get to heaven; just him and me, no one else. I love horses; I think they are magnificent animals. The Book of Revelation announces His coming and when He returns, He will be riding on a white horse. (Rev. 19:11-13 KJV).

1

TODAY'S BATTLES

Today people are taking their fight to the streets with protests to oppose policies in government. We have gang wars, drug wars, wars among nations, wars in the heavenlies, on ground and at sea. We fight battles in our sleep with nightmares and in our homes with family. We fight with our mouths and fists and tanks and nuclear weapons.

I wrote a column on August 4, 2015 about how we have increased our battles strategy to include the skies with drones and new satellites. Today we are not content with wars on the ground; we have taken it to the skies.

Prayer: Isaiah 45:8 NIV.

The hunger for world dominance has many leaders abusing their powers in government by launching missiles as a show of force. Military capabilities have gone way beyond the earth realm and into space. It reminds me of the building of the tower of Babel when God came down to take a closer look at what man was building. (Gen. 11:4-5 KJV). He is taking notice today whether we realize it or not. What kind of towers are we building today and how far do we want to go in order to achieve world power?

We are now in a new age with new technology and new weapons but God will raise a standard in the kingdom. He will never leave His people defenseless; for the word says He is our Defense.

Psalm 46:9-10 KJV: He is a God that has the power to end wars and destroy weapons. Nations should trust in His mighty hand and give Him praise. He is our stronghold!

The Accuser of the Brethren: Today we have witnessed the persecution and deaths of many of God's people by Anti-Christ and Anti-Semitism spirits who are working against God's people here and abroad. Many of them have been killed in the Middle East. The greatest character about our Father is that He will not leave us as orphans to face battles and struggles alone. One of His many promises is to never leave or forsake us. Satan goes before God to accuse the saints. (See Job 1:6-12). People who falsely accuse God's people are doing the work of the devil. According to the Book of Revelation, Satan is defeated by Jesus Christ and the blood He shed on the cross, by Believers who witness to God's truth and willingly and sacrificially gave their lives over to martyrdom. (Rev. 12:10-11 NIV).

Self-indulgence and selfish ambition have given rise to evil behavior. Mirrors will determine our fate on the battlefield. We must all first examine our own hearts before we prepare to meet the King.

There is not a weapon here on earth or in the spirit realm that can succeed against God's people and every accusation or curse spoken against us will come under judgment for this is the legacy of God's saints in His kingdom. (Isa. 54:17).

I love to pray psalms 91 and 18 for my own personal deliverance.

These two psalms are my favorite passages for praying during times of great warfare and stress.

There is so much uncertainty today about where the world is headed. God is interested in all things great and small. He does not want us to be ignorant but instead wants us to be headed in the right and only direction. He alone is our compass and knows where we should be in preparing for his coming. All of these battles are preparing us for the final battle as written in the Book of Revelation, chapters 19 and 20 NIV.

Unfortunately, battles are a way of life in this world and God is very aware of all of them; this is why He has equipped us with His armor. (Ephes. 6:10-12). Wars are not about men and flesh but against powers and principalities and wickedness in high places. God not only equips us, but fights with us and for us. We are allowed to fight the good fight of faith. This is where we find our victory.

Prayer for confidence: Psalm 27:1-3 (KJV).

The word delivers on the battlefield: No matter what comes our way, we can always stand on the Word.

Psm. 119:110 NIV – A lesson to the wise to remain steadfast in God's word.

Psm. 119:157 NIV – endurance.

Psm. 119:170 NIV – prayer and God's promise to deliver.

8

PRAYER - ONE OF OUR GREATEST WEAPONS

One of the greatest, most effective ways we can prepare for our King's coming is to pray that God's people would be positioned into high seats of government carrying out His will in the earth bringing truth and righteousness to the multitudes. Exercising our right to vote on godly issues is another way.

We are not to participate in darkness; but instead, bring God's light into it carrying His peace to all nations. Only God is able to pour out all of the love and peace that can help us live through these dark days; helping us to faithfully endure. He is our source and supply. The question is, "How desperate and in need are we to reach out and grab hold of it?"

The world has their tanks, missiles, and warships, nuclear weapons, drones, and chemical weapons but the people of God have the greatest weapon in God's arsenal, the power of prayer. It is an awesome privilege to go before His throne of grace to petition and intercede in world end time events.

The world may be able to take prayer out of schools but they will never be able to pull it out of the hearts and spirits of fervent and faithful servants of God who will humble themselves and push forward believing for and expecting and answer from God almighty. Jesus said that His house will be a house of prayer.

Jesus often went to His Father in prayer during His ministry. He also encouraged others to pray. Through the power of prayer and by the authority God has given us in Luke 10:19 and Mark 16:16-18 (GNB), strongholds will be broken because of the anointing, demons will be cast out, and people will be healed and delivered. According to the words of Jesus, prayer keeps us from entering into temptation. (Matt 26:41 KJV).

The Lord is raising up mighty intercessors all over the world who fast and pray for their own church family, missions, revival in the United States as well as internationally. A global network is now set up around the world.

The Lord showed me an open vision while in prayer one evening on Tuesday, September 10, 1996 a worldwide network with thin lines interwoven one on top of the other coming from various locations. He's placing intercessors, people in deliverance ministries, evangelists, teachers, pastors, apostles, prophets, etc. linking them together in the spirit all over the world. He placed in my spirit that the battle to come will be so intense that even though we are not in the same location in the natural, our spirits will be so linked that we will be in prayer together almost 24 hours a day all over the world. The spirits overseas will tap into our spirits here in the United States and we will be joined in prayer for the same battle. We might be in a grocery store or at work and the spirit will quicken us to pray for the same concern. He will refresh and renew us so that we will never tire. There will be prayers of agreement all over the world spontaneously, without any notice or communication with one another.

God showed me this vision in the mid 1990's of intercessors linked like a beautiful weaver's cloth –

‡‡
‡‡
‡‡
‡‡

Prayers of agreement were going forth without notification 24 hours around the clock; one city with many cities, one state with many states, one nation with many nations all over the world. (Matthew 18:19).

God also told me that our gifts will intensify. They will be strengthened and increased. For example, the gifts of words of wisdom, discernment, and the prophetic, etc. The word of God says that we should never cease to pray. (1 Thes. 5:17 KJV). As Christians, prayer is a way of life for us. This word, a year later in 2017, has come to pass. Since that time, the Spirit of God has opened up many prayer groups and ministries and has intensified our gifts; especially in the prophetic and mostly in dreams and visions as He promised in the Book of Joel. (Joel 2:28).

One morning at about 9:00 am, a sister in Christ called. She didn't know why she was calling me. She said the Lord showed her many things concerning prayer, intercession, the Holy Spirit, and scriptures relating to prayer. He even had her to read a special book on prayer the same night He gave me the worldwide vision. He wanted to confirm His word to me. I did not know what she was doing Tuesday evening and she had no idea what I was doing. God will always confirm His word. Prayer is our heart cry to God's attentive ear.

The Power of Prayer to conquer and defeat 'temptation':

The source of temptation is found in Luke 4:13 (KJV). It is the devil's handiwork. In preparing ourselves to be cleansed, we must resist temptation. Jesus said we should keep watch and pray that we may not enter into temptation. (Matthew 26:41 GNB). He said we should pray that we would not be led into temptation and ask that He would deliver us from evil. (Luke 11:4 KJV).

For even though we try not to sin, our selfish desires get in the way and the world seduces us out of righteousness and the will of God into pride, lust, and greed. Temptation is the hook and bait of Satan. Lust and greed ensnares us and tend to be the hardest to conquer. (I Tim. 6:9) .

Like a knight in shining armor, God rescues us and keeps the unrighteous for the day of punishment and judgment. (2 Peter 2:7-9 GNB). He finds a way of escape for us in I Corin. 10:13. Galatians 6:1 says we should restore those who are being tempted in all gentleness and examine our own ways lest we be tempted as well. (NIV).

Because Jesus was tempted, He is able to assist us when we are weak and vulnerable. (Heb. 2:18). Jesus was also tempted as a man yet He sinned not. He understands about all of our weaknesses. (Heb. 4:15).

Temptation is like a dark spiritual magnet that forces us to comply. We fall into temptation when we are lured away or deceived by our own lust and cravings. It is a hunger and a thirst. The Lord said if we are thirsty to come to Him. God is a holy God and righteousness is His standard for us. Jesus said we should hunger for it.

In Prayer: Faith feeds prayer to the fullest level of expectancy. We know God hears and we are assured that His will and hand will move on His timing. The Spirit revealed to me one day in bible study that this is true of "a faithful prayer life." Faith is the substance of things not seen. The gift of faith coupled with confidence in the power of prayer (I John 5:14 NAS). How do we receive such a faith? Faith comes by listening, being attentive, and believing the Word of God. (Rom. 10:17 KJV). We must, with absolute certainty, know that we believe it to be true. The word of God builds faith.

It's time for us to rise up and take back what the enemy has stolen from us and begin separating ourselves from the enemy's wiles and schemes that war against our soul and spirit. It's time for us to press into the heavenlies and get in the face of God. The church must no longer be complacent. We must possess this land for Jesus Christ!

Many times we are guilty of starting our own battles by disobeying God and by our lawless deeds. Man must have love and respect for one another's life, land, and liberty. Temptation to do harm to others brings forth consequences and retribution. Making threats is no way of regaining peace. God wants us to give the battle over to Him. Another way to overcome battles and defeat the enemy is by walking in the word.

9

WALKING IN THE WORD HELPS US TO WORK OUT OUR OWN SALVATION IN PREPARING FOR THE LORD'S COMING

God lays out all the means and tools to get us to repair and restore our lives ad relationships, yet we won't even pick up the Bible. I have a sister in Christ who has bibles and psalm books. She consistently listens to praise and worship on her car ratio, but yet she told me that her only company was beer and cigarettes. She could not pay her rent because of the expense of both and her health has suffered as a result.

We don't get it!

Unfortunately, sometimes as humans living on earth, our ears are more attentive to what we grumble and complain about rather than being mindful of the godly messages pouring out of God's heart and being healed and comforted by worshipping in His presence.

We all have to walk a straight path in order to get to our final destination. Walking with God prepares us to meet Him when He comes again. In the meantime, He wants us to have knowledge of Him here and now. Listening to His word helps us to walk in the right direction; right towards His heart's desire for us.

All of us are guilty in some sense of starving our spirits by not picking up the bible and reading God's word. We sometimes make excuses for not attending bible study, dust collects on our bibles and the word of God grows dim in our hearts and minds. Straying away from the word of God lures us closer to this world system.

The world's pathway is to please self, living in fear, sin, and despair. We look to the stars (astrology), call the psychic hotline, and go to palm readers. We blame God and others for our troubles and buy lottery tickets to find our source of supply, etc. This is not consistent with the word of God--nor does it satisfy. It is unfortunate that we only tend to serve Him out of desperation, need or convenience.

Walking in the word means "applying God's word to our daily lives, putting it into practice by living out our lives through the example of Jesus Christ, and receiving knowledge of the will of God for His call and purpose." As we look at the world today, we see war, disease, crime, etc. and we become discouraged. We find that we can no longer depend on our government, spouses, employers, family, or friends but Jesus remains steadfast; He's closer than a brother. I have good news, God Is Faithful!

The power of the word gives satisfaction, peace, wisdom, comfort, joy, hope, salvation, and much more. It opens up an invitation from God giving you permission to find out more about His character so that His will, blessings, and love pours out into your heart through you and on to others. Studying the word is like opening up the gate to His kingdom and sitting beside Him listening to His wisdom. The anointing of God flows through these pages. It reveals the truth about life, love, pain, betrayal, deliverance, and joy. It feeds the hungry, gives drink to the thirsty, strengthens the weak, gives healing for those afflicted and oppressed, and cleanses the soul. It comforts the mournful, gives rest to the weary, gives love to those who are rejected, places the lost on a pathway to hope, and gives wisdom to those who diligently seeks God.

John 1:1 – "In the beginning was the word, . . ." (NIV)

"And God said" is mentioned about ten (10) times in Genesis Chapter 1. God spoke and all of creation came into being by His word. (Gen. 1:1-31 KJV). Just as it did then, it is still doing the same today. God is the same yesterday, today and forever.

God did not create man until the 26th verse in Genesis, Chapter 1. The word (in the beginning) came first. The power of the Word should be the most important priority in our lives and in the Body of Christ. In these last days, just as in the beginning, the importance of the Word will help us to stand in prayer and in ministering to others. Walking in it and obeying it will show forth as fruit in our daily lives. Jesus said we would know one another by our fruit.

God commanded Adam and Eve in Genesis 1:28 to be responsible for the care and upkeep of the earth by cultivating the ground, taking care of the animals, and to have dominion over the fish of the sea and the birds of the air and over every living creature that moves on the ground. We must fill the earth with God's divine inspiration and multiply it by spreading the gospel to our children and those outside of the family. Most importantly, another way to honor His word is to live it. God called creation and man into being by the word of His mouth.

Over the centuries man has worshipped animals and killed them by poaching where they have become almost extinct in the wild. Today, oil spills have destroyed most of the wildlife in the oceans and seas. "Mother nature" becomes a religion of what we now call New Age. Man has abused, destroyed, and committed idolatry by living out their lives according to their own will, carnal nature, and intentions.

Children have made idols of cartoons i.e. ninja turtles, dungeons and dragons, gargoyles, etc. TV Cartoons have portrayed mischievous children acting disrespectful to their parents and others. Parents should monitor their children's activities. Children today are now apprehensive about going to school because of gun violence. We must always pray for our children and believe God to shelter them. If we cannot control our own nature, there will never be any kind of gun control. (Prov. 25:28). I also believe that even if we had gun control, there are other ways of obtaining weapons i.e. on streets, on the internet, on the black market; in addition to stealing them from gun shops.

Today, teachers are dating their students. Jesus wants us to allow children to come unto Him. Parents, teachers, etc. are to guide children to Jesus Christ without any hesitation. Love and protection begins with Jesus as Lord and Savior. Introduce your children to Him.

God will never be replaced by any being or animal, any man, or any other spirit for He has said He will not give His glory to anyone. Remember that Satan caused his own fall by wanting to be like God. The word of God says that pride comes before a fall. God resists the proud and gives grace to the humble.

In the gospel of John Chapter 8, Jesus spoke to the Pharisees and Jewish authorities. He says in verse 47 that anyone who is from the Father listens to His words. (GNB)

The word of God lasts forever –

The eternal word: Psm. 119:89 – The word is forever established in the heavens and is always in agreement with the will of God.

Guidance and Direction:

Psalm 119:105 – God's word, accepted into our hearts, directs our feet as a lamp; a light to every pathway. It works both ways: when we stray or get away from the word, when we are not in line with God's word, everything else is darkness; we stumble and fall prey to "Words" of the world and the lies of the evil one. The word is "Truth". When prideful people spread false accusations against us, God's truth sustains us as we remain faithful and steadfast. (Psm. 119:69).

How Shall We Live? By every word that God speaks to us and through us. [Matt. 4:4 KJV]

Romans 1:16 KJV – Jesus endured the suffering and shame for our salvation so we should never be ashamed of His gospel. In the gospel, righteousness from God is revealed, a righteousness that is by faith from first to last, just as it is written we all shall live by faith. Who is the righteous? The people who believe in the name and in the man called Jesus Christ. They are made righteous by what He did on the cross at Calvary. The righteous will live by faith and faith comes by hearing and hearing by the word. Guess what! We need to read, meditate, memorize, and minister the word of God in our walk of faith.

Jesus is the Living Word still revealing the thoughts of God the Father through the power of the Holy Spirit.

The Word Sustains Us:

When I hear the word sustain, I see a truth scale that balances our will with God's. He sustains us with His word of power. There were times in my life when the Lord chastised me personally or through someone else by a word of wisdom or knowledge. It made me take a good look at myself and correct my behavior. Sustain is to support when you are loaded down; to carry when you are heavy- laden; to hold when you have been shaken. He sustains the universe. (Heb. 1:3 GNB).

Just as we need food and water to sustain us so does our spirit. Our spirit must feed on the word in order to live a life acceptable to God. Satisfaction is found in Jesus' righteousness. There has to be a hunger for it. (Matt. 5:6).

Prayer: Psm. 119:116 – God sustains us with His power and promise that we may maintain and preserve hope.

The Word Satisfies:

The Book of Psalms Satisfies the Hungry Soul

I utilize this Book of Psalms as a reaffirmation of my silent prayers, worship and encouragement unto the Lord.

Psalm 22:26 NIV – The word feeds the poor and afflicted.

Psalm 63:5 NIV – When our soul is satisfied, we need to render a joyful praise to the Lord.

Psalm 90:14 KJV – God satisfies us with His mercy and joy all of our days.

Psalm 91:15-16 KJV – The Lord will always answer us in times of tribulation and; He will satisfy us, deliver us, and show us His salvation. I usually read this whole psalm out loud and walk my home for a spiritual housecleaning.

Psalm 107:9 KJV – When we are empty, He fills us and we are satisfied.

Dissatisfaction comes by selfish wants, desires, and pleasures. In life, we can't always have our own way although we try awfully hard. Proverbs 27:20 NIV says, *"death and destruction are never satisfied; neither are the eyes of man."* This world cannot completely satisfy our physical and spiritual needs. God wants His word to find its way to our hearts, to cleanse our thoughts and strengthen our walk. (Jer. 17:9-10 NIV).

This psalm is a great prayer for the nations. (Psm. 107:20 NIV).

Medical science is now saying that antibiotics once used long ago for illnesses are no longer combating some of the same illnesses today. Physicians are only humans they cannot heal everyone. Our diet and lifestyle has a lot to do with our physical condition. Jesus said he came that you may have life and have it more abundantly. He is our Healer. He is our Provider and provides for not just some but all our needs. (Phil. 4:19 GNB).

Unfortunately, we often see ourselves through the eyes of the world instead of experiencing the heart of God. God seeks the rejected, the outcasts, and the failures of this world. He knows we are imperfect and loves us anyway.

Jesus also said that in the last days men would be lovers of self. Power, greed, pride, corruption and selfish-ambition have entered into the minds of certain men and women in this world system. Government leaders today are being toppled by nations due to corruption in their official positions of authority because they do not know or recognize the Lord but instead, despise and have abandoned him. (Isa. 1:3-4). A nation is blessed when it exalts the Lord.

Everything that belongs to the world by means of selfish desires, possessions, etc. comes from the world which is passing away but he who does the will of God lives forever. (I John 2:16-17 GNB). God may have placed us here but the world is not or eternal home. We must walk in this truth.

God is our Helper while we wait and anticipate His coming.

For a spirit of depression: We must walk daily with our minds and hearts filled with God's word. Loss is one thing we never look forward to in this world and sometimes it comes suddenly without warning.

God is a God of comfort to all mourners. Instead of ashes, He gives us beauty and the oil of joy for those who grieve. When we are sorrowful, He clothes us in a garment of praise. (Isa. 61:2-3). In heaviness, the word strengthens us. (Psm. 119:28). (KJV).

The Word and its Unlimited Capabilities:

Psalm 119 is full of hope. We find that the Word of God is not only the will of God, it is one way we are able to reach Him in prayer. I pray the word of God quite often.

Blind Eyes are opened through the Word:

Psm. 119:18 – His word and commands enlightens our heart that we have clarity of vision. We will not stumble. (NIV).

The Word gives Wisdom and Understanding:

Psm. 119:98 KJV – God's wisdom through His commands supports us in overcoming our enemies if we are ever mindful of them.

Psm. 119:130 – As the word enters our spirit man, it gives insight and enlightenment; especially to the naïve. There is an increase in comprehension and understanding that develops our discernment and builds our faith.

Prayer for understanding: Psm. 119:169

Prayers for freedom from oppression:

Psm. 119:121-122 and Psm. 119:134 (NIV).

In Suffering and Affliction:

Psm. 119:67 - obedience brings healing. (NIV).

Psm. 119:107 - the word preserves us. (NIV).

Psm. 119:50 KJV – Comfort and restoration.

Psm. 119:71 KJV – The lessons we learn through our affliction.

Psm. 119:92 KJV – Salvation from perishing.

The Word brings Hope:

Years ago, the Lord told me never to say, "I hope". I now know why; because it indicates doubt in the heart of the person who says it. God is our hope; there is no need to utter this phrase. I believe that hope is an anchor that holds us steady through troubles and adversities.

What the world needs now is genuine love and hope in a Savior called by the name of Jesus Christ.

Psm. 119:49 – Have hope in His word and promises.

Psm. 119:81 – Hope for our salvation.

Psm. 119:114 – He is our secret place of protection and our Defense. Our hope is found in His word.

Mercy is a rare gift in man because it causes us to become compassionate and responsive to the needs of others.

Prayer for Mercy: Psm. 119:58

John 14:27 GNB – The world defines peace in human terms. Peace Is a free gift of God given as an inheritance. We should never be troubled or afraid.

For Peace: Psm. 119:165 NIV – For those who love God's word, it not only pours peace in their hearts but it also keeps them from falling into temptation or sin.

In the Book of Psalms, the Lord covers us with His protective hand. For all who are oppressed, we can count on God to be our Refuge. [Psm. 103:6].

10

THE IMPORTANCE OF THE WORD AS THE SPIRIT LEADS

The word is alive and active in the earth in the person of the Holy Spirit. The Spirit searches everything even the hidden depths of God's purpose. (I Corin. 2:10-13 GNB). He helps, comforts, and empowers us here on earth while we await our King. The Holy Spirit not only fills us but prompts us to move as God wills.

The Holy Spirit of God fills us with His power in activating and demonstrating His gifts. He is our Helper and aids us in revealing His truth to those who are lost. He equips us in preparing the lost so that they will have a full increase in His wisdom and knowledge of His truth. It is God's way of opening up a door for the lost to receive Him when He comes.

Earlier I spoke about how the Holy Spirit gave me revelation through the word. The more I read, the more He pours out to me a deeper, clearer understanding of what God is saying through scripture. I always tell people to pray for revelation before reading the word. The Spirit of God told me not to separate the Spirit from the word. We need the Spirit's revelation; after all, He wrote the book. (John 14:26 GNB).

The more you read the word, the fresher and newer it becomes in your spirit. There are many times when we question people's motives and their actions. Honesty is a rare trait these days; the word of God is the only truth that removes all dishonesty so that you are able to discern good from evil.

The word of God works through obedience

Obedience: The meditation and study of God's word keeps us from being rebellious and unrestrained. We become like an unmovable root ever growing and increasing in strength and righteousness. (119:10-11 NIV).

The book of Luke, chapter 11, verses 27 and 28 thoroughly and completely reveals to us how important God's word is and how Jesus publicly acknowledges it. A woman raised her voice in a crowd and said to Jesus that He was blessed by the womb that bore Him and the breasts that He sucked! Jesus replied back to her that the true blessing lies in those who not only hear the word of God but those who obey and practice it. In I Sam. 15:22 KJV, the prophet Samuel said, *"..to obey is better than sacrifice."* Obedience gives us a resting place that falls into unison with the will of God.

One day as I was walking in downtown Houston about to attend a company seminar, the Lord spoke to me and said, "In order for you to be effective in the gifts I have given you, I require love and obedience." I told him I would try. Just to know the word of God is not enough, we must obey. Obedience is the most effective way to grow and please God the Father.

Even when we know God's truth, we sin anyway and when results of conflict, troubles, and afflictions come our way, we blame God for them. We become foolish in our thinking. This is why the word says we are to examine ourselves. (Lam. 3:40 NIV).

Jesus sets forth qualifications for being a true disciple which extends to His word. He said we must abide in it and that we are to have knowledge of His truth because it sets us free. (John 8:36). The word "abide" has several meanings: (1) to endure under pressure; 2) to believe and comply; and (3) to live in. We buy a home, dwell in it, and plan to stay in it for the rest of our lives. We find our home in the word of God. It is where He abides. It is where He speaks to our heart. There's an old saying, "Home is where the heart is." Does your heart abide in His word? The word of God should be our dwelling place and the dwelling place for our children. It helps us to persevere and endure the conflicts of this life on earth.

We can so easily become slaves to sin (John 8:34 NIV); but Jesus is the "Living Word" and if the Son liberates you, then you are truly free.

A most important advantage of the word: Jesus Christ talks about being the true vine and we are the branches. We are to bear fruit and He will prune. Branches become fruitful when they are severed. We have a greater measure of faith and our lives become richer and fuller with God's correction and instruction. (John 15:1-3).

Paul encourages us to believe and desire the word of God, not as the words of men, but as it is written. The word of God is successful and fruitful inside of all those who truly believe.

2 Tim. 3:16 GNB:

1. The breath of God, His character and will is in scripture. It is divinely inspired instructing us in all truth.

2. Scripture yields rewards in learning and application.

47

3. It admonishes and corrects our sinful nature.

4. It instructs us in righteousness so that man is made whole and complete; capable and accomplished; and adept in every good work.

The word of God can truly change lives. By walking in the word we receive satisfaction, healing, deliverance, guidance, and wisdom; and by preaching the word, others receive the same blessings.

The Word of God prepares the world to experience God intimately, to desire Him passionately, and to be in readiness for when He gathers His church for His second coming. This is why it is so important to abide in the word. If you put God's word into practice and obey it, the world will know that you are truly one of His disciples.

Another powerful description of the word is found in Heb. 4:12 GNB. God's words is life and full of power; it is like a sharp two-edged sword, piercing and apportioning out the breath of life and spirit, joints and marrow judging the thoughts and purposes of the heart. Discernment is the greatest gift of God that shields us from lies and falsehood.

11

HANDLING THE WORD OF GOD

E very word in the bible is tried and proved. We are never to add to the word of God. (Prov. 30:5-6 KJV). We are also never to subtract from the word. (Rev. 22:18-19; Deut. 4:2 KJV).

Over the centuries, the word of God has been misused and abused by false teaching or through selfish gain but no one can ever destroy its divine truth and unlimited treasure filled with the Spirit of God's revelation for mankind. On the other hand, it has transformed the lives of people all over the world whose hearts were willing to receive Jesus Christ as their personal Lord and Savior. They are His witnesses in the earth.

We can have knowledge of the word and still choose to not walk in it. We can also have knowledge with no wisdom or understanding. We need to pray for God to help us. The Parable of the Sower demonstrates how we receive God's word in our hearts. (Matt. 13:1-9, 19-23 NIV). The seed is the Word. We must get out of the bondage of self and pursue godliness for a better world planting seeds of righteousness in the hearts of men. When the world is out of control, its peoples must practice self-control (restraint) which is one of the fruit of the Spirit of God. Ask God for His fullness, the fruit of self-control, and a Spirit of wisdom and understanding.

We receive the word like a bank deposit. We keep it in our heart and take it out as the Spirit leads on an 'as needed basis'. It often comes to us as a means of being a witness to others, to preach in due season, to evangelize, or to prophesy. When the account is almost empty, we go back to the word to get more treasure. The Lord never runs out of revelation and His treasure house is always within reach. We can be selfish and hoard it (never use it) or we can give an account to God as He instructs us on how to make more when the account is empty. Just as we have a responsibility to give an account to God, we are responsible and accountable on using the word accurately as a good steward in His kingdom.

A pure heart and genuine love for the Father and the lost helps us to facilitate the word accurately. A passion and desire for God's word to reach the nations and our own heart helps as well. Everything is pure and increases in the hands of God, our universal King.

12

PERSONAL REVELATIONS FROM THE HOLY SPIRIT

Over the past few years, the Holy Spirit has given me a better understanding of the scriptures.

Teamwork: Matthew 11:29 – Jesus wants to be joined with us at the neck; where the yoke is placed. The neck holds the head to the Body. Jesus is the Head of the Body of Christ. He wants us to learn from Him and partake of His divine nature and there, we will find rest and comfort. Our lives will result in producing good fruit.

The Spirit of God told me to look up the word "Yoke" in the dictionary. It means to labor together as a team. He explained to me that it was all right for me to surrender my burdens to the Lord but I must also work together with God. For example: standing firm in the faith, being patient, glorifying God in the earth, trusting God, praying and believing God for the answer to prayer, obeying God's word, etc. "We are God's fellow workers . . . ". (I Corin. 3:9 NIV).

God's revelation in Romans 8:1 One day the Lord gave me wisdom about the word 'condemnation'. The Spirit explained to me that this goes all the way around. We are not to condemn others, others are not to condemn us, and we are not to condemn ourselves. He also said, "Do you know why there is no condemnation?" I said, "No Lord". He then brought me back to the book of (Genesis 1:31). He said, "There is no condemnation because after the Lord created everything He made, He said, "It was very good."

Burden Bearers: The Lord spoke to me once again when I was going through a difficult time in my marriage, experiencing poor health, and trying to solve a few financial problems. He said to me, "Everyone must carry his own cross. I carried mine alone but you have the Word, the Holy Spirit, and each other."

The Holy Spirit reveals the word of God in such a way that no human can. How can we obtain this revelation? Choosing to become intimate with the Word and experiencing a personal one-on-one relationship with the Lord Jesus Christ.

Walk in the Spirit and you will not fulfill the pleasures of the flesh. Learn from His teaching and walk with Him daily.

13

GOD OUR TEACHER AND EXAMINER

Both the righteous and the wicked are tested by God and Psalm 11:5 KJV says that He hates those who love violence. God examines our hearts to see if we are truly His. He wants to know all that fills our heart. (Hezekiah/2 Chron. 32:31). No one in this world has your best interest at heart like our Savior. He is the Author and Finisher of our faith and He is where our true tests begins and ends. When we enter into any relationship, we are interested in every aspect of that person's life and character. We want to now the depths of knowledge of who that person really is before we commit to a permanent relationship. God wants the same from us.

God tests us but we are never to test Him. The people of Israel sinned and rebelled against God in the desert and put God to the test by asking Him according to their own appetites and selfish desires. (Psm. 78:18).

There were many times in my life where God showed me visions of being in a schoolhouse. In later years, He showed me in the spirit realm wearing a graduation cap and carrying a diploma. I knew what this all about; my growth and learning from His word speaking into my life. He wants to examine the deepest parts of who we are in Him as true Believers.

Test of Obedience: We observe this life through God's relationship with Adam and Eve. They received the word of God to not eat of a certain tree in the Garden of Eden but they failed their test miserably. Their error was in not being obedient. Disobedience tells God that we cannot be trusted and; according to our own standards, He cannot be trusted. On the other hand, God is always faithful, ever true. He desires the same from His children.

Test of Faithfulness: Abraham was tested in the area of faithfulness. When God told him to offer up his son Isaac as a sacrifice, He was really asking Abraham, "Do you love your son more than you love Me and will obey My word and commands?" Of course we know that Abraham's son was saved and that God provided a lamb in his place. (Gen. 22:1-14 NIV and Hebrews 11:17 GNB).

Moses was tested on courage and endurance: God turned his staff into a snake and told Moses to pick it up; He made his hand leprous and restored it back to health. He then sent him back to Egypt where they wanted to kill him but God spoke a word that it was safe and encouraged him to go on. God then chose Moses to deliver His stubborn-stiff necked people out of Egypt where they complained for 40 years in the wilderness about Moses and their stomachs. Our physical and moral appetites will sometimes trip us up.

Samson was tested on self-control. Lust for women and the things of this world.

The Apostle Paul was tested on his willingness to have knowledge of God and in that knowledge sacrifice all for the sake of Jesus Christ. The word tells us to make our lives a living sacrifice holy and acceptable to God. When faced with a prison conviction, Paul had no interest in human judgment or that of his own, for God was his only judge. (I Corin. 4:1-4 GNB).

The Word of God is Tested: (2 Samuel 22:31 NAS).

Job was already proven to be committed and faithful but God tested him before Satan, the accuser. Satan wanted God to prove this word even if Job had to lose everything including his health in life. This is one example of the word of God being tested for God told Satan that Job was faithful. Job was tested on proving his devotion to God and to His word; devotion through endurance. Job even had friends who made his condition ever more intolerable but in the end, Job prayed for his friends and all was restored.

While writing this book, I asked the Lord why His word had to be tested. Sometimes we just want to hear from Him. The Lord instructs us as a Teacher who gives lessons to their students and then tests them to see if they really learned or retained what was taught. It is alright if they fail because they are allowed to take the test over again until they aspire to reach a higher level of wisdom, knowledge and understanding. If they are diligent and patient, they become a valuable member to society. God will get us where He wants us to be; more like Him. After all, He is our parent. It is in testing us, that He qualifies us for an even greater work in His kingdom. We excel in having a more excellent spirit ready to be used by the Maker.

God teaches us how to test the spirits in I John 4:1-3 GNB and He also chooses testers as He did Jeremiah. Jeremiah was to test and evaluate God's people. (Jer. 6:27 NIV). God's Spirit works with us in the mission field.

We need to look inside our hearts and evaluate our own actions and walk of faith. (2 Corinthians 13:5).

God's Fire is another testing ground:

In Matthew 3:11 NIV, John the Baptist said *"he baptized with water for repentance."* He continued to reveal that Jesus had an even greater baptism; by the Holy Spirit and fire. We are all fire walkers whether we know it or not. We will walk in spiritual fire and be tested but God is there to take us through it. It is through this baptism that we are really proven to be true Believers.

The Hebrew boys in Daniel were tested in the fire and passed their exam in Daniel 3:8-30 KJV. In the end, the King caused Shadrach, Meshach and Abed-nego to prosper in Babylon and came to the realization that their God was God and blessed His name. Our testing ground gives testimony to the knowledge of God to those who are perishing and does not know Him personally.

In Zechariah 13:9, nations like Israel are tested by God. God refines us like fire and tests us like gold in order to take us through a cleansing process that would restore us back into a rightful union with Him. Teaching and instruction requires testing and examination.

After we have graduated and, if we make it that far, He prunes us and sharpens us as iron in the fire. (John 15:2 GNB and Isa. 48:10 KJV).

This is my own observation. Before we pick fruit from trees, we patiently wait for its season to mature, and then we examine it to see if it is ripe enough to eat. The purpose for planting trees is to provide for our physical needs in reaping its harvest. We then wash the fruit and eat it. Everything in life goes through a process of growing. God helps us to work out the fruit of patience and endurance.

As Christians, our process is walking closely with the Lord and producing good fruit by taking in the milk of the word until we are able to eat meat. God then purifies us and uses us for His service.

Before we invite people into our home, we must know who they are and whether or not they are a Believer. Many deceivers who do not believe in Jesus Christ have gone out into the world. God wants to prepare us to live in His eternal home. He needs to know if He can trust us with what He has already given to us and does not want us to lose what we have already achieved through His wisdom and counsel.

The precious Holy Spirit, His gifts and callings, and His plan and purpose are available for us today. Invite Him in. God is the righteous way for man to follow. In Psalm 26:2 (KJV), David asked God to test him as a reassurance of his own devotion and walk before the Lord. Will we make the grade? God has a standard and He lists them in His word. His Son paid a great price for our salvation so naturally He does not want us to take advantage of His mercy and grace. He is interested in every aspect of our lives. We must be found like Him—to be trustworthy.

14

SEEKING THE LIVING AMONG THE DEAD

D uring the time of Jesus' ministry, a woman came to Him with a vial of perfume, wept and anointed His feet. When people called her out as being a sinner, Jesus said she was preparing Him for burial. The Lord knows when it is a time for preparation.

In Luke 24:1-9, women were on their way to the tomb of Jesus Christ carrying spices after His crucifixion. When they found the stone rolled away from the tomb, they went in and did not find his body. They were greatly confused as to where the body was laid. Then behold, two men stood by them in shining garments. They were so afraid, they bowed their faces to the ground and the men asked them why they sought out the living from among the dead. Jesus was not in the tomb because He had risen from the dead.

Many times, without even realizing it, we are doing the same thing in a way. Jesus is alive and we are living as though He was dead. Jesus told John when He doubted he was alive that blessed are those who believe and have not seen Him physically.

Do we seek people who are dead in Christ for answers when they don't have the answers for themselves? All of the answers we will ever ask in life are written in the word of God. When I recommend people invest in a bible to find answers, they are pleasantly surprised when they find them. Seek Him for yourself.

Some people would rather go to the graveyard and talk to the dead rather than talk to a Living God. You will not get a response or an answer there; it is dead and buried. Isaiah 65:1-4 (NIV) says they are people who *"pursue their own imaginations."* The dead will receive their reward on judgment day just like the rest of us. They have already had time to prepare. Whether they make it to heaven or not, only God knows.

God requires us to work out our own salvation right now among the living. He wants us to share His good news among the living. He is a God of the living.

In these last days, we must ask ourselves the following questions:

1. Are we really seeking the living God or some kind of facsimile (a copy of likeness of one)?

2. Are we guilty of seeking wisdom and counsel from people who are dead in Christ?

3. Are we guilty of turning away from God and falling under the influence of the occult and dark powers, false religions and doctrines?

Jesus warns us in Matt. 24:23-25 (KJV) that people will say to us, "Here is the Christ." We are not to believe them because false prophets will arise in these last days and will demonstrate many signs and wonders. We must be mindful to know God's truth for ourselves because even God's own people may possibly be deceived. I have already seen this today in the media, in a few churches and in politics. How then are we to know? If God's truth is not in us, we are open to deception. This calls for another question, "Do you believe in God and are truly walking in His Word?" Deception cannot abide in the place of God's truth. We must not be quick to believe every spirit that manifests itself as an angel of light.

Darkness and death are synonymous. The only way we will be able to distinguish God's light from darkness is to seek His face, confess our sins, repent, and live a life worthy of His love and forgiveness. This is the greatest and only way we can prepare to receive our coming King. We are alive in Christ from death and dead works and to die is gain according to the apostle Paul.

What is death? Death is the wages of sin which is already in the world. The spirits of Anti-Semitism and Anti-Christ are already operating in this world and many are being attacked, being imprisoned and killed for their faith. (I John 2:18-23 KJV). We are not to call good evil and evil good. Sin reverses God's order and definition but God's truth, confession, and repentance gives us true enlightenment. We are not to fear but instead be encouraged, watch and pray; knowing that the Lord's coming is at hand. For Jesus said He is the resurrection and the life and whoever believes in Him shall live even if he dies. (John 11:25-26 KJV).

People are fleeing death from terrorists groups in the Middle East, Africa, etc. They are frequently moving into other nations. The word of God in Isaiah tells us to say to those with a fearful heart to take courage, God will save you. He will make a highway called, 'The Way of Holiness.' (Isa. 35:4, 8 NIV). We should flee lawlessness and sin the way we flee terror. I pray that these nations which are welcoming in these migrants will carry God's truth in their hearts and share His gospel from His heart to every refugee.

We are not a perfect people. If we were, we would have no need of a Savior. Jesus is the answer. He is the problem solver, peacemaker, way maker, and devil shaker and it is He and He alone Who delivers. Freedom from the cares of this world comes from the Father.

Rev. 2:10: We are to remain faithful until death, for Jesus said,

"He will give us the crown of life." (NIV). Are we faithful in living out His word? It's not just about reading or memorizing the word. He is calling His church to live out His word. Seek Him and He will work it out. He will pour out His love, His power, and His comfort whenever you need it. He is life to us.

In May of 1993, the Lord gave me a vision of being raptured up; and as I looked down, I saw thousands upon thousands of people who were still left upon the earth who were not saved. I cried out to the Lord and tears ran down my face. I said, "Lord what can I do?" He truly showed me His heart. Will you be among those numbered in the New Jerusalem in Revelation 21:1-7? (KJV)

I have a brother in Christ whom, together with three (3) other brothers, spent their lunch hour on Thursdays in a street ministry with the homeless giving out bibles, praying for the lost, and preaching the word years ago. They preached the message of salvation to both children and adults in an area of the city where there is a spirit of despair and hopelessness. They brought Christ, our hope of glory. They were preparing a way for people to know the Lord before His second coming.

God is calling us out in these last days to choose life and not death. The message as spoken in Isa. 55:6 rings clear for us. It says we should continue to seek the Lord now while He can be found and speak to Him while He is near. The broad path is filled with people who seek their own selfish desires and not that which gives life to our body, soul, and spirit. Choose to be made whole, choose redemption in the name of Jesus Christ, and choose life.

Who are we seeking today? I pray with all my heart that it is the Risen Lord!

15

EARTHLY WEALTH VS ETERNAL RICHES

A re we seeking earthly treasures instead of Jesus, the one and only treasure worth finding; the soon and coming King? There are people who hoard wealth which can be stolen or when they die, no one is there to spend it.

Jesus is the source of our supply. (Phil. 4:19 GNB). What are we to seek? The word of God says first and foremost we must seek the kingdom of God. Worldly possessions can become an object of idolatry if you allow yourselves to be opened up to the worship of such things. As children of the King, we must use Godly wisdom.

It is a blessing to be rich; we come into error when we seek riches instead of God. This is how God define riches:

- We must be "rich in *good works" and "be generous" in heart*. (I Tim. 6:18 GNB).

- God is rich *in mercy and great love*. (Ephes. 2:4 GNB).

- We must *hold to the richness of His word*. (Col. 3:16 KJV).

16

A PEOPLE OF HERITAGE
AND INHERITANCE

G od has been preparing us to be a holy people since the time of Adam. He is still preparing us today and always as we await His return. He desires a Bride without blemish. Are we cooperating? In order to know who we are in Him, we must first know who we are not.

Although we live in this world, we are not of this world. We are seated in heavenly places with Christ Jesus. In I John 2:15 the word tells us not to love this world nor the things in it because in it is lust of the eyes, flesh, and pride. All these things are not of God. Unlike other men, God's people do not suffer from an identity crisis. We know who we are in Him through Jesus Christ. We are His righteousness in Christ Jesus and He will judge this world by His righteousness. (Psalm 9:8 NIV).

We are the adopted sons and heirs of the Father through the Spirit of God. (Gal. 4:4-7 KJV). We come in all sizes, shapes, and colors because God does not discriminate. We are all of one mind and belief and spirit. We are one with Him in love and acceptance.

Just as God has chosen us, we must choose Him. Everything that God is, makes His divine nature ours for the choosing. He is love and so we should love.

"You must be holy because I am holy." (I Peter 1:16 GNB).

We are set apart for God and God alone in faithfulness and commitment. The world loves its own and the reason why most people hate Jesus Christ and His people is because He has chosen us out of this world as people unto Himself. (John 15:19). Jesus warned us in scripture that because of His name, we will be hated among men. (Matt 10:22).

We are not to be yoked with unbelievers. In Ezra 9:1-2, God's people joined into relationships with foreign nations. God has specific laws and commands concerning diet, morality, penalties for idolatry, etc. Foreigners did not live under these same laws and commands. They would soon fall under the influence of foreign cultures and beliefs. God is a jealous God. This word is still true today. We are not to associate or be joined together with unbelievers. Light opposes darkness and righteousness opposes lawlessness. (2 Corin. 6:14-15 NIV). We are to love them, preach, and give witness to the gospel of salvation but not fall under these false beliefs.

Through my experience in ministry, I have witnessed Christians who marry unbelievers and the marriage very seldom worked out. The apostle Paul states that when we are married, we seek to please our spouse. This was the case with King Solomon when he married women who practiced idolatry and sacrificed to other gods. God took a portion of his kingdom from him when he fell under their influence. We serve God alone and only come under the submission of His will and commands.

We must first know Who He is before we can identify with whom we are in Him. I Peter 2:9 declare that we are –

A Chosen Race: God's choice of people who are all related by common spiritual descent, united by a common history—Jews and Gentiles related through Christ Jesus.

We are God's handiwork; a people created and chosen for Him.

Royal Priesthood: In Hebrews 5:5-6 and Psalm 110:4, He is a High Priest according to the Order of Melchizedek. Jesus Christ is Ruler of the nations over all the kings of the earth. He created us to be priests in His kingdom to God the Father. When we accept Him as King and Savior, we become children and heirs to His kingdom and according to Exodus 19:5-6, through obedience and covenant relationship, we are a kingdom of priests.

A Holy Nation: We are under God's sovereign government and inclusive of all who believe in Him. As Believers we are all apart of God's DNA which includes living a holy life. We are made holy through the sacrifice of Jesus Christ but must not take advantage of His grace by abounding in sin.

Deut. 7:6 and 14:2 – We are a holy people chosen to be solely for God's own possession and He disciplines us so that we may continue to increase in a life of holiness. (Hebrews 12:10 GNB).

Peculiar People and God's Possession: Malachi 3:16-18
God distinguishes between the righteous and the wicked; the one who serves Him and one who does not serve Him.

The people of God are different in ways the world does not understand. We are able to hear the voice of God and enter into His presence; eternal life is our inheritance and He promised that we shall never perish. In 2018, Vice President Pence was ridiculed because he said he hears the voice of God. A woman said he was mentally ill. He responded with an answer from the word of God. He said, God's sheep hears His voice. (John 10:27 KJV). We are God's treasured possession; particular and distinct.

We are not to resemble the world or desire anything of this world. We should not place anything of this world above God. We are His treasure in earthen vessels and we carry His word and commands in our hearts. Our paths lay in the way of righteousness, truth, and an eternal home at the end of days.

As God's own possession, He is called Adonai (Owner) of all that was, is, and is to come. We are the sheep of His pasture where we are cared for and protected by the Great Shepherd. He upholds and sustains us.

We are His Lights in a Dark World: Those who follow Him shall never walk in darkness. (John 8:12 GNB). We are transformed from darkness into His light; from the old man to the new. He wants us to shine our light before men. (Matt. 5:14-16 GNB). He enlightens our soul and spirit that we may carry on His light in speaking His truth to the nations. Light guides and opposes darkness. Light brings revelation of things past, present, and things to come. We walk as children of the light. (Ephes. 5:8 GNB).

17

THE PROMISE OF THE HOLY SPIRIT AND GIFTING FOR TODAY

Wе are a people who hold and release the gifts of the Spirit as the Spirit distributes and prompts us. The Holy Spirit is given unto us forever. He is the Spirit of truth and reveals God's truth to us. The world cannot receive what they refuse to believe and think they know. He is our Helper. (John 14:16 GNB). Is the Holy Spirit in you?

It is not enough to just request a gift and not be responsible or accountable for that gift. Accountability comes with acceptance. God said if we love Him, we will keep His commandments. We are not to use His gifts for profit. They are not for sale.

"Every good gift and every perfect gift" comes from God, our heavenly Father (James 1:17 KJV); and the gifts and callings of God are complete, conclusive, and unchangeable.

I don't know about you but I want all that my Father in heaven has to offer. The word of God says we are to pursue love and have a desire for His spiritual gifts, especially that of prophecy. (I Corin. 14:1 KJV). Prophecy moves with God in demonstrating to us His destiny for His kingdom. It is a spiritual compass pointing the way to His coming. The spirit of prophecy is the witness and testimony of Jesus Christ. (Rev. 19:10 KJV).

God's Laborers in the Field

Until the Lord's return, He requires us to remain active in gathering souls for His kingdom

The Spirit of God imparts and distributes these gifts. They are listed in I Corin. 12:8-11: Words of wisdom, words of knowledge, faith, gifts of healing, working of miracles, prophecy, discerning of spirits, tongues, and interpretation of tongues. (NIV).

The Fivefold Ministry Gifts to edify the Body of Christ are listed in Ephesians 4:10-13: They are Apostles, Prophets, Evangelists, Pastors, and Teachers.

In 1975, the Holy Spirit led me to buy my own personal bible. I began reading it. Next, God led me to start fasting; I was living in Boston, Massachusetts at the time. After a few months, God spoke to me and said I was to move to Houston, Texas and not look back. I have lived here ever since. Although I accepted Jesus Christ as my personal Lord and Savior and continued worshipping on the Sabbath, my spirit was hungry for more of God.

I continued in the old lifestyle of sinning and going to church until I received the Holy Spirit. My whole life really began to change. I started studying the word and attending bible studies and He began opening up ministries for me (Prison Ministry, Worship Ministry, and Altar Ministry). Through the prayers of others and my heart being opened to His fullness, I eventually received His gifts as well. (Acts 15:8-9).

God began testing me in these gifts when I was working at an oil and gas firm. He then moved me into giving people I did not know in restaurants a word of wisdom and knowledge. They confirmed the word I spoke from the Lord and told me that they were seeking God about the same issue. I then graduated to the great congregation.

Now there are many people today who say that the gifts died with the apostles so as to say Christ is dead. Since God is alive, so are His gifts. Free yourselves from the doctrine of men which are futile and ineffectual. We are not to be lured into human philosophies, deception, or man's tradition. (Col. 2:8). Tradition invalidates the word of God. (Matt. 15:1-6 NIV).

A really true relationship requires two people. We see the relationship Jesus had with the Father. The truth of the matter is that God is all about relationship, not religion. There are times when I just want to shut the world out and just read the word and get into praise and worship. It is during those times that God is either healing my wounds or giving revelation through His word. Jesus often left his apostles to commune with the Father.

People who do not believe in or understand the Spirit of God will have a difficult time understanding spiritual truths. (I Corin. 2:12-15 NIV).

18

PARALLELS OBSERVED

I have observed that there is a parallel of some of the lives of the people of the Old and New Testament.

Moses and John the Baptist - God used Moses to free His people from bondage and slavery in Egypt so that they could enter into the Promised Land. When God opened up the Red Sea, He also opened up His heart and Law to His people. Some believed, others doubted and all complained. God chose Moses to open up a way for His people to receive His laws and commands, set up His tabernacle, and to have them enter into worshipping Him on His Mountain. John the Baptist preached repentance and baptism in order to free people from sin (bondage). He prepared the way by announcing the first coming of our Lord and King, Jesus Christ and opened up a way for baptism and repentance.

Joshua and Jesus - Jesus is one of the Greek forms of the Hebrew word Joshua; it means "Savior." He saved us from our sins. Joshua finished the work of Moses and led the people to the Promised Land. Jesus completed the work of John the Baptist after repentance and baptism by giving the people the word, ministering healing and deliverance, dying for our sins, and leaving the Holy

Spirit as recorded in John 14:15-17. He gave us the promise of the Holy Spirit.

Moses gave Joshua the responsibility of continuing to lead God's people into the promise land. What Moses began, Joshua finished. Where the first Adam failed, Jesus (the second Adam) succeeded. Jesus, through His death on the cross, paid our pardon and we in turn gained eternal life with the Father. Just as Jesus said on the cross, it is truly finished.

God will return and gather His people in His second coming. (I Thes. 4:16-18 GNB).

19

THE WORD FOR HEALING AND DELIVERANCE (POWER AND DEMONSTRATION)

Jesus promised in Mark 16:17-18 that **Believers** will be given power and these signs will follow. They will drive out demons (deliverance ministry) in my name; they will speak in strange tongues; if they pick up snakes or drink any poison, they will not be harmed; they will lay their hands on sick people, and they will be healed. Over the centuries we have heard thousands of healing testimonies from people, including myself, who have experienced the healing power of Jesus Christ. [Testimony: Decades ago, the Lord healed me from scoliosis and a lesion in my breast]. When I was a teenager, a doctor spoke a curse over me that I had sickle cell anemia and I would not live passed the age of 30. I will be 70 years old this year. God is able!

The Book of John says Jesus is the Living Word. The word of

God has been healing man since the time of Jesus Christ. He is the same yesterday, today, and forever. He is our victory over sin and the grave and all sickness and disease.

Faith is the key that unlocks your miracle:

Faith is a gift from the Spirit of God. (I Corin. 12:9 NIV). In the Book of Matthew, the faith of a certain centurion caused him to believe Jesus could heal his servant only by speaking the word. Jesus marveled at his faith and the centurion's servant was restored to health at that very moment. (Matthew 8:5-13 NIV).

Our faith, trust, and confidence in the Lord shall heal our bodies; without it is impossible to please God. (Luke 18:42 and Heb. 11:6 GNB). It is also written in James 5:15 that the power of faith and prayer will heal the sick and God shall raise them up and restore them. Faith must stem from the person laying hands and the person being prayed for—iron sharpens iron.

Psalm 103:2-3 is my favorite prayer for the sick. It is the promise of God for forgiveness in iniquity and healing diseases.

Jesus Christ also raised the dead and delivered many people from demons. He had both a healing and deliverance ministry. When a Canaanite woman came to Jesus to ask that He deliver her daughter, Jesus said that deliverance was the children's bread. (Matt. 15:21-28 GNB). Deliverance encompasses all of healing in any and every form; including that of people being possessed by demons.

20

JESUS' PARABLES. THE INVITATION AND HOW WE ARE TO PREPARE

When Jesus said, "The Kingdom of Heaven is compared to" in these first two parables, He was calling us unto Himself in covenant relationship; He gave us a divine look into His kingdom; He tells us what is required of us so that we will be dressed and equipped to receive Him when He comes.

A Divine Look at the Kingdom through the Parables of Jesus Christ

*An Invitation to **the Wedding Feast** –* Matt. 22:1-14 KJV

A king invited guests to a wedding feast for his son. He sent out his servants to those who were invited but they refused to attend. They were too busy with their own agendas. Others attacked and killed his servants (Christian persecution and martyrdom). The king was angered and sent his armies to destroy the murderers. He then told his servants that those who were invited were not worthy; so he sent the slaves out once more to the highways to anyone who would accept.

The servants invited both good and evil guests and the wedding hall was filled. When the king arrived, he saw a man not dressed in wedding attire. He asked him why he came without wedding garments and ordered the servants to bind him and cast him into darkness. The king then said that many are called but few will be chosen.

Will we accept the Lord's invitation to enter into His kingdom? How will we be dressed in appearing before the Lord at the end of the age?

Compared to The Ten Virgins who went out to meet the Bridegroom: (Matt. 25:1-13). Ten virgins took their lamps and went out to meet the Bridegroom. Five were foolish and took no oil with them for their lamps. The Bridegroom was delayed but when he came out to meet them, the foolish virgins asked the sensible, more vigilant five who had oil for in their lamps for some of theirs. They replied with a no and told them to purchase oil for themselves. Those who were ready went into the wedding feast but unfortunately, the door was shut by the time the other five arrived with their oil. They begged for entry but the Bridegroom said He did not know them.

Oil is a symbol of the Holy Spirit. In Old Testament times, oil was used for preparing food (food is also spiritually discerned as the Word of God). God's lamp is the symbol of life that holds the light of God from within and His presence. We are to watch and be on the alert for no one knows the hour of His coming. As we examine ourselves, we must be sure that we have oil in our lamps in joyful readiness to meet our King.

The oil in some of the virgins' lamps went out because they did not prepare for the Bridegroom's coming. The anointing of God and His Spirit is symbolic of His light inside of us. We carry His light in preparation for His coming. We must not be negligent and let His light go out in our spirit during these last days. Timing! Will it be too late for us to enter into God's kingdom or will we be prepared?

Compared to a man who sowed good seed in his field (Matt. 13:24-30 KJV). Jesus' parable of the wheat and the tares is a prophetic look into the end of the age. The one sowing the good seed is the Son of Man and the world is the field. The reapers are the angels. The tares (sons of the evil one) were sown alongside the wheat. The devil is the sower. At the end of the age, the tares will be harvested and burned up. They are the men of lawlessness. He will then gather the wheat into his barn.

We are God's planting upon the earth—a harvest for His kingdom. The tares are sown by the evil one, whose crop at the end of the age will be gathered by God's angels and thrown into everlasting fire. Our evil deeds will become evident at the end of the age but why wait until it is too late?

21

DRESSING THE BODY OF CHRIST

The Lord spoke to me one Sunday while I was in prayer with a few intercessors. He said, "Man is concerned about marriage, restoration, and finding a spouse." He said to me, "The only marriage I am concerned about is the marriage supper of the Lamb. Prepare my people to receive my son!" I pray this book has done just that.

I thought about the word of God which declares that the House of God is where judgment begins. (I Peter 4:17 NIV). It continues to say, "... *if it begins with us, what will the outcome be for those who do not obey the gospel of God?*"

Before we talk about getting dressed, let's see what God's word says about "nakedness" and what it really means and how God clothes and covers us.

Exposure

Everything is laid bare before the eyes of God. We must realize that nothing is hidden from God. (Heb. 4:13 GNB). This is the key to being prepared; a pure heart before God. He knows the motives of the heart as He examines it carefully.

Nakedness:

How do we define nakedness? When we look at these definitions, we see ourselves wanting and in need to satisfy our nakedness in this life. Many of us see bare relationships, bank accounts, etc. We want to dress ourselves in fine clothes and enjoy the world's possessions. The word of God, as I said earlier, satisfies. It satisfies our nakedness in this life; not in the way of earthly possessions, but peace and contentment.

Fear comes with nakedness. We fear lack and exposure (especially in regards to sin). When Adam disobeyed God in the Garden of Eden, he feared God's voice and presence. (Gen. 3:10).

Nakedness as Shame

Nakedness as a sign for the prophet Isaiah and evidence against Egypt and Cush. (Isa. 20:1-6).

Israel's chastisement: God can strip away, expose, and make bare. (Please note the chastisement of Israel in Hosea 2:1-5).

Nakedness as disgrace: When we look at our neighbor's nakedness rather than our own. (Hab. 2:15-16).

Nakedness shall not separate us from the love of Christ. (Rom. 8:35).

We must allow God to hold us accountable by His testing that we may be clothed in white. (Rev. 3:18).

Blessed are those who are awake and hold and retain their garments that they may not be naked and exposed. (Rev. 16:15 NIV).

When In Lack

People scatter and become prey for the enemy without a true Shepherd. A true Shepherd has the Lord's compassion and heart in seeking the lost and seeing to the needs of the Lord's sheep. A true Shepherd protects his sheep from predators.

I was shopping in Sears one day buying a gift for my pastor. A salesman with grey hair said to me, "We have enough pastors, what we need are more shepherds." His words touched my heart. The Lord is our shepherd; we shall not lack for anything. (Psm. 23 KJV).

God watches and weighs the hearts of man. He warns that the ways of a wicked man will not only trap him but he could also die from a lack of correction from the Lord. (Prov. 5:21-23 NIV).

When Unarmed and Defenseless

- God provides the armor that we are able to stand against the evil one. (Eph. 6:11-17).

- Our Help is in the Lord. I should know from my own experience. Psalm 121 has been and still is my favorite memory verse and prayer.

- God is our Deliverer. (2 Peter 2:9). He rescues us from temptations and trials. He knows how to keep the ungodly under correction and discipline until the day of judgment.

Clothing in scripture:

God's grace to the unfaithful: How God gives life, washes and cleanses, and adorns in beauty. Jerusalem is covered in His grace. (Eze. 16:1-14).

22

GARMENTS OF THE OLD TESTAMENT AND NEW TESTAMENT

Now let us go back to the beginning and see what the first garments were in Genesis 3:21. God gave Adam and Eve garments of skin. Symbolic of God's provision in covering our sin, guilt, and shame making us suitable and acceptable to enter into His presence.

Earlier in this book, I spoke about the importance of being dressed properly before the return of Christ in the book of Matthew. This scripture in Exodus is a type of consecration and washing of clothes in preparation of going before the Lord's presence. (Exodus 19:10-11).

Jacob gives his son Joseph a coat of many colors described as being long-sleeved and ankle length. (Gen. 37:1-3). I believe this was a prophetic sign that he would eventually obtain a high position. This sign came to pass years later. I see the colors as different races of many nations. Because of Joseph's dream interpretation, nations were saved from the famine.

The Lord clothes us with "garments of salvation" and "robes of righteousness." (Isa. 61:10 KJV). He encourages Jerusalem in the kingdom age to clothe themselves with strength and beautiful garments. (Isa. 52:1 KJV).

God sees purpose in all of us. This vision was to reestablish the priestly office to Israel through a spiritual cleansing. Joshua's filthy garments were removed to take away his iniquity. A clean turban was placed on his head as well as festal robes. (Zech. 3:1-5).

The Lord chooses our battle gear: God has a special anointing and gift of armor for each individual. King Saul saw David as being too young for battle so he offered him his armor. God tests and proves each of us in a specific skill and task. David refused Saul's armor. (I Sam. 17:33-39).

Torn Garments

A symbol of God's judgment in I Sam. 15:12-28 NIV. King Saul tears away a piece of the prophet Samuel's robe after Samuel rebuked him for rejecting the word of the Lord. Samuel said God would tear the kingdom away from his hands.

Also, in the Old Testament renting or tearing clothes was a sign of mourning. Some examples are found in Genesis 37:34 and Job 2:11-12.

Clothing as it relates to passing on the anointing:

Elijah transfers his mantle to Elisha in 2 Kings 2:9-14. A mantle is a robe or cape worn by prophets (some biblical sources say it is a veil as well). It is God's chosen garment specifically given by divine design exclusively for one individual. It can either be worn or transferred. In this particular case, Elisha requested a double portion of Elijah's anointing from his mantle.

God's cloth of Fine Linen :

- In ancient times, linen was made from flax. Clean linen represents the righteous acts of the saints in Rev. 19:6-8.

- Symbolic of promotion. Pharaoh placed garments of fine linen on Joseph. (Gen. 41:42 KJV).

- In the New Testament, Joseph brought a linen cloth to wrap the body of Jesus which is a Jewish custom for burial. (Mark 15:46 KJV).

Spiritual Clothing:

- Deception by False Prophets: The meaning of sheep's clothing. (Matt. 7:15 KJV).

- We must be clothed in humility. (I Peter 5:5 KJV).

- A woman's spiritual virtues: Women's Clothing which includes but not limited to a benevolent and charitable spirit; a blessing to her husband; she is clothed with strength and honor; she wears and creates fine linen. (Prov. 31:20-25). Personally, I see women as the center of a home serving every member of the household. The colors mentioned in proverbs are scarlet and purple. I see scarlet as a symbol of blood, sweat, and tears poured out from her heart in serving her family as well as others and I see the color purple as richness in serving as Queen submitting herself under the authority of her Lord and King Jesus Christ.

- The importance of internal adornment is for a wife to be in submission to her husband and in obedience to the word of God. (I Peter 3:1-5).

- Clothed with power from on high (Holy Spirit). (Luke 24:49 and Acts 1:4-5 GNB).

- Sackcloth and Ashes: Clothing to remove anguish. (Esth. 4:3,4).

- Forbidden clothing: (wearing clothing of the opposite sex). (Deut. 22:5).

The Lord's clothing –

The Lord comes to judge and save: He will put on righteousness as a breastplate; salvation as a helmet; garments of vengeance and arrayed with zeal. (Isa. 59:16-18 NIV).

Christ's Second Coming: In Revelation 19:11-14, the Lord wore a robe dipped in blood and His armies were clothed in clean white linen. (NIV).

Healing flowed through the hem of Jesus' garment. (Matt. 9:20-22 KJV).

23
THE SACRIFICE
OF PRAISE

I personally believe that praise and worship keeps us in our place; a place of being humbled before God in a position of gratitude for all that He has done. We are always selfishly looking for ways to catch God's attention in sickness, trials, or whenever we have a need. Well here is a revelation—God always desires our attention as well. I envision sacrifice as time and attention given to God. It is not only genuinely given through devotion but a lifetime of commitment. Loving and praising God to me is not a sacrifice but a privilege and a necessity. A marriage match made in heaven to share God's heart song. (Heb. 13:15). Praise and worship is all about place and position—away from us and this sinful world and into God's holy presence and glory.

My second ministry was the Worship Ministry in the Church of Christ. I must say that this was the most rewarding ministry I have ever had. Little did I know that this ministry would touch my heart so deeply. The pastor prepared sermons and gave them to me so that I would be able to incorporate hymns and prayers preparing and completing the whole order of service on Sunday morning. At one point, I even got the children involved.

"How often should we praise God?" The word says, <u>continually</u>. Why wait until we get to heaven to praise God? Let's prepare to shout, sing, dance, and rejoice. Let us usher Him into our presence right here on earth.

What are we birthing spiritually?

Desire is a fire that is birthed when we hunger for something or someone we cannot live without. Prayer: God, eternal Lord and King, I lay myself humbly before your throne of grace asking you to take my heart into your hand placing a deep desire inside to worship you in spirit and in truth. Let the Spirit of Truth take hold of me and convict me of my past transgressions. Help me to seek holiness and truth. I desire to have a spirit that is always and forever stretching towards the heavens in joy and in exultation of all that you have done for me. I ask this in Jesus most holy and precious name. Amen. (John 4:24).

In order for praise to be birthed, we must have a passion and love for the Lord beyond that which is found in this physical world. It is easy for us to love someone who loves us and fall in love with someone and eventually enter into a marriage covenant. The truth is, we are already in a marriage covenant, a covenant with a great and mighty God, a King. How does our love for man compare to our love for a God who gave us the gift of life, everlasting life? Man will always disappoint, but God's mercies are new every morning. His love and faithfulness is forever. So should our praises be.

One sure way to cast out the enemy from our midst is to lift up the name of Jesus Christ. Satan cannot stand in the midst of praise. As the world faces God's judgment, the evil prince and ruler of this world will be cast out. God draws us to Himself every time we lift Him up higher. (John 12:31-32).

Why should we praise God? We praise Him because He sent His Son to die for our salvation. He sent Jesus, His Living Word and gave us the precious Holy Spirit as a guarantee and eternal inheritance. Salvation is the best reason in the world to praise God. Jesus spoke of His death and because of His death, burial and resurrection; we can boldly go before His throne of grace in prayer and worship.

Praise and worship is the Lord's dwelling place and where the Spirit of the Lord is, there is liberty and freedom.

Deliverance Comes from Praise

In Battles: Jehoshaphat won a battle through praise and worship. I spoke of battles earlier. Now is the time for all of us to open up a way of praise for the Lord to help us fight them. Let's look at Jehoshaphat's prayer which is found in 2 Chron. 20:5-12 and listen to the Lord's reply through Jahaziel in 2 Chron. 20:14-17. Deliverance comes forth through prayer and praise. (2 Chron. 20:20-24 KJV).

Joshua and the people of Israel praised God while they walked around the walls of Jericho and the walls fell giving them victory. There is victory in the praise! King David was a psalmist with a harp and a heart of worship. He won many battles against the Philistines throughout his lifetime. King David was a king and psalmist who knew how to praise the Lord. Even in his darkest hour, when his enemies were about, he praised God.

In Prison: Prayer and Praise are synonymous. Prayer and praise gives you entrance into God's throne of grace so let us go boldly and enter into His gates with thanksgiving and His courts with praise. Prayer and praise brings deliverance. In Acts 16:22-26, Paul and Silas were set free from prison.

Praise brings freedom from all struggles and distractions in life.

For comfort and a spirit of heaviness: Praise releases joy for the grieving soul. Grief is for a moment when praise comes out of the spirit.

On a more personal note, praising God delivered me from the spirit of depression and despair. I was in poor health and received a bad report from the doctor; almost lost my job, and was going through a divorce all at the same time. I told a good friend in the ministry during one of my fiery trials; I said, "I may not have anything else but I still have my praise." I did not lose that; and, because I hung on to the praises of my God, the Lord healed my body and my emotions. He is ever present working on my behalf in every area of my life.

Prayer: Psalm 42:5-8

When we get so caught up in the cares of this world and our own grief, a gray cloud hangs over us. Jesus is light and praise turns on the spotlight. He gives us the garment of praise for heaviness and despair. Jesus knows all about grief. (Isa. 53:3-11).

One Sunday in July of 1995, the Lord imparted a word to me for the body of Christ. He said, "My Father made the Sabbath as a day of rest for my people. When they are weary from battles during the week; when they feel unclean, they will come and be cleansed."

I offer praise to God on a daily basis. I am determined not to let the angels and saints outdo me either here on earth or in heaven. If we can't praise God here on earth, what will we do once we get to heaven?

We should not only praise God in song; we should also give glory and praise in declaration as a testimony to others about His awesome greatness. As people of God, we honor Him in praise; we glorify him in praise.

Did you know that every breath we take is a gift from God? Praise Him for being alive and for His precious Spirit.

We love it when people praise us and give us compliments. Humans boast in one another's accomplishments and seek rewards. God has done more for mankind than any human possible. There is a worship song which tells us to forget about ourselves and just worship Him.

When do we praise? As I said earlier, offer a sacrifice of praise continually, always and on every occasion (good or bad). Psalm 42 is one of my favorite night time offerings to the Lord.

God is able –

Psm. 147:1-6 KJV: God builds up and gathers together His people. He heals broken hearts and binds wounds. God has great power and infinite understanding. He lifts up the humble and casts down the wicked.

Psm. 148 – Angels and all the heavens and earth give praise to our God.

Continuous praise replaces the exaltation of ourselves, others, and material possessions. No one and nothing holds our soul's salvation and redemption in this life or the next but our one and only true Lord and Savior Jesus Christ.

Worship –

• Acknowledges God's presence in our lives. Worship pleases, honors, and glorifies Him for who He is, a God who is worthy.

- Keeps us humble. John the Baptist praised the Lord in this way. He said he must decrease and Jesus increase. (John 3:30 KJV).

- *"Come near to God and He will come near to you."* (James 4:8 NIV).

- Brings us to a place of freedom in the spirit that takes us away from the cares of this world.

- Brings joy to the spirit during times of heaviness and grief.

- Delivers us from life's battles and puts us in a place of rest in the heavenlies.

This is my personal song - Psalm 146.

We should meditate about His love and goodness and His grace that helps us to endure. The Father's love is above the heavens and is beyond measure; reach for it!

PRAISE THE LORD!

Finally – In examining ourselves, (Isa 56:1-2 NIV).

a. Enact godly laws and live by them.

b. Remember to always congregate and assemble your-selves on the Sabbath Day.

c. Live a godly life with clean hands and a clean heart.

All of these ingredients make up the recipe that prepares us to usher in and expectantly welcome our soon and coming King: A bride that has been cleansed by the word and is obedient to it; A bride that ministers the word to the lost as well as the body of Christ; A bride who is prayerful; A bride who seeks her groom continually and hungers for His wisdom; A bride who is not easily deceived and tests all things; A bride who worships the Lord in spirit and in truth and finally; a bride who is dressed for the occasion.

We were born to be lights in the sky and on the ground with a twinkle in our eye walking with God Who is ever nigh. I want no sad bad ending in my life story; only God and His hope of glory.

The Lord's word on February 27, 2017: He said, "I have hidden treasures that are yet to be revealed in prophecy. They are for My faithful remnant. Be attentive to My Spirit, and stay in readiness. I lift up My people to help them to stand and feed them My word to demonstrate My light in the earth. Be prepared My people to move when I say move and speak as the Spirit prompts. My work in the kingdom is gearing up with My armor and equipment. You will have the faces of the glory to come. You will be the instruments of My peace."

Moving Forward –

I was born in the same year Israel became a nation (1948). I am blessed with this great legacy and thank God for calling me out to serve His kingdom in this age; this age and time that Israel is celebrating its 70th anniversary and the United States moved its embassy to Jerusalem where the Lord has placed His name. (2 Chron. 6:5-6). I see this as a sign that the God of Israel is pointing the way for His coming.

As a child of the soon coming King, I plan to show Him my devotion and have Him as my lifelong companion. I want to minister His word with grace and gentleness and worship Him continually. Although He is in my heart, my eyes will always look upon the heavens joyfully awaiting His magnificent arrival.

For some, it is so hard today to accept and give encouragement to anyone but I gladly would like to encourage every man, woman and child today to willingly leave behind all of the heartaches and pain; all of the disappointments and failures of the past and ready themselves to greet our King together with all of the angels and saints. Hold steady to God's plan for your life with Him until He returns to gather you to live with Him throughout all eternity.

The Lord's word on May 26, 2018 –

"My Son's blood was not spilled in vain. Salvation has come and is for all who live in this world. Hear the sound of keys opening up prison doors. Hear the Lord's voice saying, "I have prepared a way for you." Job lost all of his possessions and family that was closest to his heart yet he glorified God. This world is slowly fading away so now is the time to prepare yourselves by being born again into a new life with your Savior. Man's desire is not God's desire. It is never too late to set the world on fire with His heart of compassion and His desire for you to feast at His table. His word creates life and brings divine order to the universe. We must start to prepare now, in this age as the time is getting near to His return."

Heavenly choirs are singing as the crescendo rises. The excitement is building as we prepare ourselves to meet our King!

A Special Invitation
THE WEDDING FEAST

In Louisiana, growing up in the Catholic Church, we believe that each nun is married to the Lord. Jesus reconciled us with the Father and was one with us on the cross of Calvary bearing the burden of our sins. Each and every one of us on earth has a great part in accepting this covenant of marriage to the Lord. Our relationship with Him binds us to His divine love and commitment. Each and every one of us in the Body of Christ represents His bride. Jesus Christ is the Groom who woos us and calls us to Himself.

I believe that weddings symbolize new beginnings; a new beginning that gives us a new eternal life of love and joy. Throwing rice began in ancient Rome. Rice is symbolic of fertility. When our family and friends throw rice on the bride and groom, they are expecting and hoping for a family increase. Marriage encourages expectancy; a multiplication of other future marriages through children.

From generation to generation: God is all about increase and advancing His kingdom. His bride feeds the world with His word and uses His word to clean house. His word trains and teaches children how to obey.

Hear the invitation and enter in –

"The Spirt and the bride say, "Come!" and let him who hears say, "Come!" whoever is thirsty, let him come; and whoever wishes, let him take the free gift of the water of life." (Rev. 22:17 NIV).

www.ingramcontent.com/pod-product-compliance
Lightning Source LLC
LaVergne TN
LVHW052034080426
835513LV00018B/2320